NATURAL PHENOMENA

SINKHOLES

by Eric Reeder

FOCUS READERS

WWW.FOCUSREADERS.COM

Focus Readers is distributed by North Star Editions:
sales@northstareditions.com | 888-417-0195

Produced for Focus Readers by Red Line Editorial.

Content Consultant: Robert Brinkmann, Professor of Geology, Environment, and Sustainability, Hofstra University

Photographs ©: Christian Gooden/St. Louis Post-Dispatch/AP Images, cover, 1; a katz/Shutterstock Images, 4–5; Tami Freed/Shutterstock Images, 7; kenez/iStockphoto, 9; Michael Szoenyi/Science Source, 10–11; Red Line Editorial, 13; Northern Imagery/Shutterstock Images, 15; Konstantnin/Shutterstock Images, 16–17; corbac40/Shutterstock Images, 19; Michael Warren/iStockphoto, 21; Matyas Rehak/Shutterstock Images, 22–23; Nicole S Glass/Shutterstock Images, 24; Carol M. Highsmith/Carol M. Highsmith Archive/Library of Congress, 26; Jad Davenport/National Geographic Creative/Alamy, 29

ISBN
978-1-63517-912-5 (hardcover)
978-1-64185-014-8 (paperback)
978-1-64185-216-6 (ebook pdf)
978-1-64185-115-2 (hosted ebook)

Library of Congress Control Number: 2018931716

Printed in the United States of America
Mankato, MN
May, 2018

ABOUT THE AUTHOR

Eric Reeder is a writer and editor. He has published articles on various subjects, and he has written and edited educational materials. In his spare time, he enjoys swimming, going to the beach, collecting antiques, and spending time with his family and friends.

TABLE OF CONTENTS

CHAPTER 1

A SUDDEN COLLAPSE

Cars drive along a busy street. Then a traffic light turns red. The drivers come to a stop. As they wait for the light to turn green, the ground begins to move. Dirt and pavement collapse. A large hole opens up, blocking three lanes of traffic. Part of the sidewalk falls into the hole. So does a car that was parked nearby.

Streets had to be closed after a sinkhole opened in Brooklyn, New York.

Fortunately, no one is hurt. But there is a hole in the middle of the street. A sinkhole has formed.

Sinkholes are bowl-shaped holes in the ground. There are thousands of sinkholes around the world. They can be many sizes. Some are as small as 2 feet (0.6 m) across. Others can be hundreds

UNDERWATER SINKHOLES

The deepest underwater sinkhole ever found is in the South China Sea. It is in a coral reef near the Paracel Islands. Scientists used underwater robots to see how deep the sinkhole was. It was 987 feet (301 m) deep. More than 20 kinds of fish were discovered inside it.

The Great Blue Hole is a large underwater sinkhole in the Caribbean Sea.

of feet wide. Sinkholes can even form underwater.

Sinkholes happen when bedrock collapses. Bedrock is the layer of rock that is below the surface of the land.

For a sinkhole to form, the bedrock must be a type that can be dissolved by **groundwater**.

Many sinkholes form in limestone. This rock dissolves easily. Holes and cracks form in the rock as it dissolves. Eventually, these holes and cracks connect together. Water can flow through the rock and form even bigger holes. Over time, the flowing water wears away the bedrock. When the bedrock under the top layers of land dissolves, the land collapses. A sinkhole opens.

This process often happens over a long period of time. But some sinkholes form very quickly. Buildings can fall down as

Several cars fell into a sinkhole in Mississippi.

the land caves in. Animals, houses, and cars can fall into the hole. In rare cases, people have even been swallowed by sinkholes. However, most sinkholes are too small and slow to be dangerous.

CHAPTER 2

WHAT CAUSES SINKHOLES?

There are three main types of sinkholes. Dissolution sinkholes form slowly. For this reason, they are not usually dangerous. They happen in places where bedrock is not covered by much soil or plant life. Water from **runoff** and rain seeps into the bedrock. The water flows through small holes in the rock.

Water from rain eroded limestone bedrock to form this sinkhole in Switzerland.

Over time, the water dissolves the rock. It creates an underground hole. This hole causes a dip in the ground to form. Sometimes the dip is lined with rocks or dirt. These materials trap water from rain and runoff. Water collects in the dip. A pond forms.

Cover-subsidence sinkholes form in places where bedrock is covered by sand. The sand seeps into the holes in the bedrock. This causes the surface of the land to sink down. A dip forms. As more sand seeps underground, the dip grows. However, this process happens very slowly. It may take hundreds of years for a cover-subsidence sinkhole to form.

TYPES OF SINKHOLES

DISSOLUTION SINKHOLE

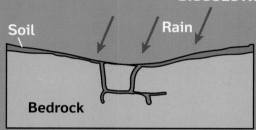
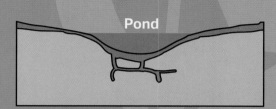

COVER-SUBSIDENCE SINKHOLE

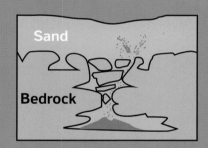

COVER-COLLAPSE SINKHOLE

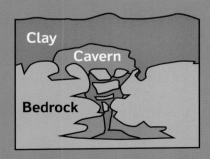

In both these kinds of sinkholes, the ground bends to form a bowl shape. It may never break apart or cave in. For this reason, these sinkholes are not always easy to spot. Some are too small to notice.

In contrast, cover-collapse sinkholes often form quickly. They happen where bedrock is covered by a thin layer of sediment or rock. The bedrock beneath this layer dissolves. A **cavern** forms. If the thin layer of land breaks apart, a sinkhole opens.

Cover-collapse sinkholes can form in just a few minutes. As a result, they are the most dangerous. This kind of sinkhole

The Konya province of Turkey has several cover-collapse sinkholes.

can swallow cars or damage buildings. Deeper cover-collapse sinkholes are more dangerous.

Most cover-collapse sinkholes are not very deep. But some can be huge. One sinkhole in Alabama is 120 feet (37 m) deep. It is 325 feet (99 m) long and 300 feet (91 m) wide. This sinkhole is sometimes called the Golly Hole.

CHAPTER 3

ON THE LOOKOUT

Sinkholes can happen in many places around the world. But they are more common in certain areas, such as places where the bedrock is limestone. Sinkholes also tend to form near other sinkholes. And they are most likely to form in a type of land called karst. This land is made of rock that can be dissolved by water.

Sinkholes form near the Dead Sea when underground salt dissolves.

GREAT SITES FOR SINKHOLES

The rock that makes up karst has many gaps in it. Water runs through these gaps. Over time, the water wears away the rock. This process creates more holes. It also forms underground caves and streams. As more holes form, the bedrock becomes weaker. It eventually collapses, and a sinkhole opens.

In the United States, sinkholes are more common in some states than in others. Alabama, Pennsylvania, Missouri, Tennessee, and Texas tend to have more sinkholes than average. Sinkholes are most common in Florida.

People who live in areas at risk for sinkholes can hire scientists. The scientists try to figure out whether a sinkhole will form on the person's land. They look for warning signs. Dips, slopes, or cracks in the ground often appear before a sinkhole. Or small ponds may form after it rains.

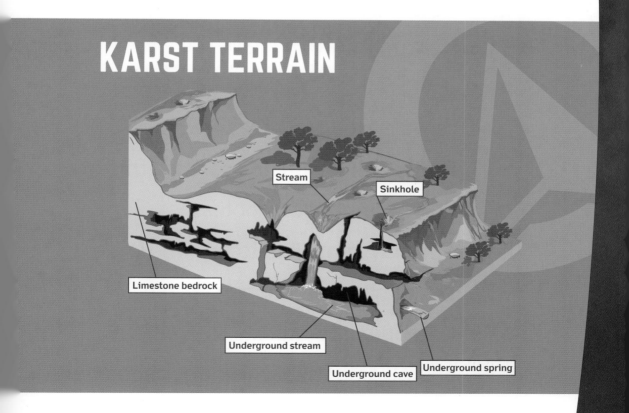

KARST TERRAIN

Stream

Sinkhole

Limestone bedrock

Underground stream

Underground cave

Underground spring

Sinkholes can form inside buildings as well. Uneven or warped floors can be signs that a sinkhole will form. So can cracks in walls or floors.

Scientists also watch the ground for movement. In one method, NASA scientists fly a plane over an area. They use **radar** to make an image of the ground. They repeat the same flight later on. In this way, they can measure how the ground has shifted. They can use this information to predict sinkholes.

It is not always possible to tell where or when a sinkhole will happen. Some sinkholes happen too quickly to predict. But in general, scientists can warn people

A sinkhole forms near homes in Florida.

if a dangerous sinkhole is about to form. Some people have had to leave their homes when sinkholes developed near them. However, most people will never be in danger because of a sinkhole.

CHAPTER 4

LIFE INSIDE

Sinkholes support many kinds of life. This is especially true of sinkhole ponds. The ponds can form in several ways. Some sinkholes have caves near the bottom and soil at the top. Sometimes the soil falls down into the cave. Then the top of the sinkhole fills with water.

A cenote forms when limestone bedrock collapses and exposes a pool of water.

Large sinkhole ponds in Florida are home to alligators.

In other cases, rocks or dirt at the top of a
sinkhole catch and hold water.

Sinkhole ponds are important parts
of many **ecosystems**. In Missouri, for
example, sinkhole ponds are part of

wetlands. Wetlands are areas that have a lot of moisture, such as marshes or swamps. Turkeys and deer come to sinkhole ponds for water. Toads, frogs, and salamanders use the ponds for feeding and breeding. Wood ducks live there as well.

Sinkholes also provide a cool, wet place for plants to grow. Plants in sinkholes often have long, thin roots. The roots can reach through small cracks in the rock around the sinkhole. Mosses and ferns grow in sinkholes, too.

Sometimes animals fall into sinkholes. They become trapped and die. Then their remains are preserved as **fossils**.

Fossils of American bison were found in a sinkhole in Wyoming.

Scientists dig or dive in sinkholes to reach the fossils. They have found remains of many plants and animals. They study the fossils to understand the plants and animals that lived long ago.

One underwater sinkhole in Mexico held fossils of a giant sloth. Giant sloths are now extinct. But several **species** used to exist. The sinkhole had preserved a mostly complete skeleton. It was from a species of sloth scientists had not known about before. Scientists tested the sloth's bones. They believe it lived approximately 10,000 years ago.

ALL KINDS OF LIFE

A sinkhole can contain many different fossils. One underwater sinkhole in the Bahamas had more than 20 species of birds inside. It also had fossils of a tortoise and a Cuban crocodile. In addition, scientists found the remains of flowers, twigs, fruits, and leaves. They even found bones from snakes, bats, lizards, and humans.

UNCOVERING ARTIFACTS

Scientists have also found **artifacts** in sinkholes. These objects fell into sinkholes many years ago. They were slowly covered up by sediment. The sediment preserved them. Scientists study these objects for clues about how people lived long ago.

Scientists found artifacts in an underwater sinkhole in Florida. The sinkhole was 200 feet (61 m) wide. It was 35 feet (11 m) deep. Scientists performed dives to explore it. They found several objects. Scientists think the objects are approximately 14,500 years old. This find proved that people lived in Florida at that time.

One object was a knife. It was made from stone and **mastodon** bones. Another was a biface. This stone tool had been sharpened on both sides. Ancient people may have used these tools to get

Scientists found pieces of a clay pot inside a sinkhole in Belize.

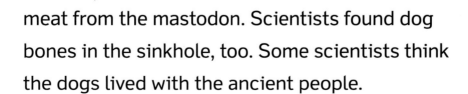

meat from the mastodon. Scientists found dog bones in the sinkhole, too. Some scientists think the dogs lived with the ancient people.

FOCUS ON
SINKHOLES

Write your answers on a separate piece of paper.

1. Write a sentence summarizing the main ideas of Chapter 2.

2. If it was safe, would you want to visit a large sinkhole? Why or why not?

3. What kind of sinkhole forms in places where bedrock is covered by sand?
   - **A.** a dissolution sinkhole
   - **B.** a cover-subsidence sinkhole
   - **C.** a cover-collapse sinkhole

4. Where would a dissolution sinkhole be most likely to form?
   - **A.** in an area that gets heavy rain and has bedrock filled with many holes
   - **B.** in an area that gets lots of snow and has thick, solid bedrock
   - **C.** in an area that gets very little rain and has bedrock made of limestone

Answer key on page 32.

GLOSSARY

artifacts
Ancient objects made by humans.

cavern
A large hole in a rock.

ecosystems
The collections of living things in different natural areas.

fossils
Parts of an animal or plant that remain preserved in rock.

groundwater
Water held underground in the soil or rock.

mastodon
A large, hairy animal that looked similar to an elephant and is now extinct.

radar
An instrument that locates things by bouncing radio waves off them.

runoff
Water from rain or snow that flows along the ground until it joins a river or stream.

species
Groups of animals or plants that are similar.

TO LEARN MORE

BOOKS

Higgins, Nadia. *Sinkholes*. Vero Beach, FL: Rourke Educational Media, 2015.

Orr, Tamra B. *Studying Sinkholes*. Ann Arbor, MI: Cherry Lake Publishing, 2016.

Squire, Ann O. *Sinkholes*. New York: Children's Press, 2016.

NOTE TO EDUCATORS

Visit **www.focusreaders.com** to find lesson plans, activities, links, and other resources related to this title.

INDEX

Answer Key: 1. Answers will vary; **2.** Answers will vary; **3.** B; **4.** A